ABDO Publishing Company

FISH & GAME

LARGEMOUTH BASS

Sheila Griffin Llanas

visit us at
www.abdopublishing.com

Published by ABDO Publishing Company, PO Box 398166, Minneapolis, MN 55439.
Copyright © 2014 by Abdo Consulting Group, Inc. International copyrights reserved in all countries. No part of this book may be reproduced in any form without written permission from the publisher. The Checkerboard Library™ is a trademark and logo of ABDO Publishing Company.

Printed in the United States of America, North Mankato, Minnesota.
112013
012014

 PRINTED ON RECYCLED PAPER

Cover Photo: GEORGE GRALL/National Geographic Creative
Interior Photos: Alamy pp. 7, 9, 22, 25, 29; Corbis p. 15; Engbretson Underwater Photography
    pp. 1, 5, 11, 13, 16, 21; Getty Images p. 27; iStockphoto p. 23; Neil Klinepier p. 12;
    Thinkstock p. 19

Editors: Rochelle Baltzer, Megan M. Gunderson, Bridget O'Brien
Art Direction: Neil Klinepier

Library of Congress Cataloging-in-Publication Data

Llanas, Sheila Griffin, 1958- author.
  Largemouth bass / Sheila Griffin Llanas.
    pages cm. -- (Fish & game)
  Audience: Ages 8 to 12.
  Includes index.
  ISBN 978-1-62403-108-3
 1. Bass fishing--Juvenile literature. 2. Largemouth bass--Juvenile literature. I. Title.
  QL638.C3L53 2014
  799.17'73--dc23
                    2013027633

Contents

Largemouth Bass!

There are several species of black bass. One of these is the largemouth bass. The largemouth bass is native to North American waters.

Bass is the most popular freshwater sport fish in the United States. Each state keeps track of its biggest catch. In 1987, a 16-pound, 8-ounce (7-kg, 227-g) largemouth was pulled from Alabama's Mountain View Lake. The Minnesota state record is an 8-pound, 15-ounce (4-kg, 425-g) fish caught in Auburn Lake in 2005. A recent record-breaker came from Oklahoma's Cedar Lake in 2012. It weighed 14 pounds and 12.3 ounces (6 kg and 349 g).

Largemouth bass are not easy to hook. Once caught, they are fighters! With sudden strikes and airborne leaps, they give anglers a thrilling challenge. No wonder largemouth bass are so fun to fish!

In 2011, 10.6 million American anglers cast a line for black bass. The largemouth bass was the most desired species.

History

Black bass are one of about 30 species in the sunfish family. One of the black bass species is the largemouth bass. There are two subspecies of largemouth bass. They are the northern largemouth bass and the Florida largemouth bass.

All black bass are native to North America. The largemouth bass is native to the eastern United States. Over time, it was introduced into new **environments**. Today, the fish is found in waters worldwide.

For centuries, fishing helped North American coastal tribes survive. Native people caught fish with nets and spears. In the 1700s and 1800s, European immigrants entered the wilderness. Anglers fished as much as they wanted. By the 1890s, this was reducing fish populations.

Increasing the number of bass by fish farming would not work. Bass must **spawn** naturally. And, they will only eat live food. So, the bass population had to be managed in the wild to keep it in balance.

Largemouth bass are the largest members of the sunfish family.

In Balance

Today, officials work to preserve the natural **environment**. To this end, each state manages its waterways. Officials estimate the average age, size, and number of fish in a body of water.

To do this, the fish are identified, weighed, and measured. Then, they are returned to the water. With the collected data, states set limits on the number of fish a single angler can keep. They also set length limits.

The **bag limits** on bass don't just protect the bass population. They manage other fish, too. For example, laws may limit bass to fish between 12 and 15 inches (31 and 38 cm). This leaves enough large bass to eat smaller fish species that may be overwhelming an **ecosystem**.

In addition to bag limits, each state has its own procedures for issuing fishing licenses. Fortunately, many

Some states collect data by electrofishing. Biologists temporarily stun the fish with an electric charge. They place the fish in a tank that keeps them alive. After recording data, the biologists return the fish to the water.

anglers are happy to follow the rules. Often, the more people enjoy fishing, the more they enjoy learning about fish!

Mouth to Tail

A typical largemouth measures 15 to 18 inches (38 to 46 cm) in length. Females measure 24 inches (61 cm) long. Males usually grow to 15 inches (38 cm).

In cold water, bass grow slowly. Northern largemouth bass weigh about four to five pounds (1.8 to 2.27 kg). Six pounders (2.72 kg) are considered trophies. The Florida largemouth bass grows faster in its warmer native waters. It can reach up to ten pounds (4.54 kg).

As you may have guessed, the largemouth bass has a large mouth! When it is closed, the fish's upper jaw extends past its eye. In comparison, the jaw of the smallmouth bass stops at the eye.

Largemouth bass are also called bigmouth, bucketmouth, and hawg.

The jaw of a smallmouth bass does not extend past the eye.

The largemouth has a dark green back and a silver belly. A horizontal black stripe runs along each side. The gills and body are covered with a protective slime.

Largemouth bass have **calcified** bones in their skeletons. This makes them fast swimmers. So do their fins. Besides the tail fin, they have three lower, two upper, and two side fins.

All fish have a swim bladder. This is an air sac in the belly. Filling it with oxygen allows the fish to float. Releasing the air causes the fish to sink. This allows a bass to control the depth and water temperature at which it floats.

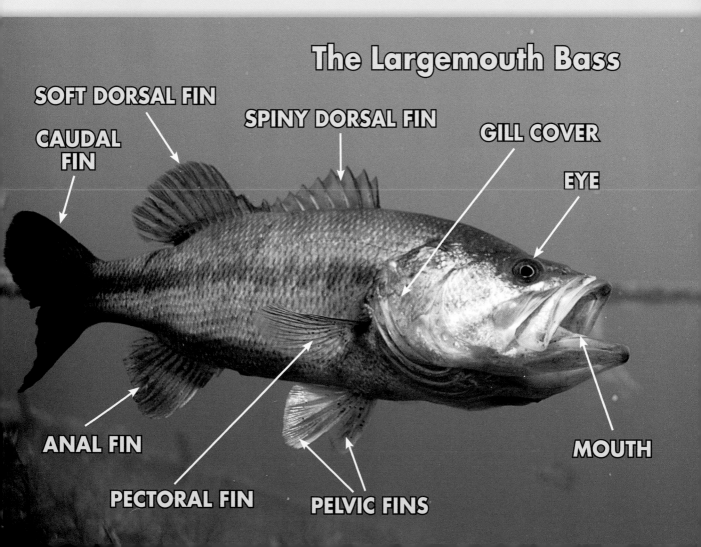

The Largemouth Bass

SOFT DORSAL FIN

CAUDAL FIN

SPINY DORSAL FIN

GILL COVER

EYE

ANAL FIN

PECTORAL FIN

PELVIC FINS

MOUTH

Senses

Largemouth bass have clear vision in a range of 10 to 15 feet (3 to 4.5 m). With eyes set far apart, they see objects off to their sides. They can also see above, below, and almost behind them!

Bass can see color too. They can see red and violet best. Green is also easy for them to see. They can even see colors up above the water's surface.

It looks like a largemouth bass has no ears. But, the fish's ears are inside its head behind its eyes. Sound waves strike the fish's **lateral line**. These vibrations travel to the fish's inner ears.

Studies have shown that bass use their senses to make judgments. With their sight, hearing, and touch, they inspect an object. They decide if it is dinner or

WILD FACTS!

The citizens of Minnesota buy more fishing licenses than those of any other state.

danger. Underwater cameras have captured bass swallowing lures and then spitting them out! They swim away, while the anglers holding the rods never even notice.

A bass's eyes do not adjust to filter light. So when the sun is very bright, a bass will seek a darker place in which to float.

Habitat

Largemouth bass are not found in rapids or swift rivers. They prefer calm, fresh waters. Lakes, ponds, streams, and slow-moving rivers all make good bass **habitats**.

Largemouth bass keep a small home range. Some never travel more than 200 to 400 feet (61 to 122 m). They might move if disturbed by storms, **climate change**, or human actions. But mostly, they stay in one place.

Largemouths like to have a getaway plan. So they float near drop-offs, rocks, fallen trees, or sunken boats. Weeds such as water lilies, cattails, or bulrushes also provide good hiding places.

North America

Europe

Asia

Africa

South America

Australia

Where largemouth bass live

N

Uneven lake bottoms contain many perfect bass hideouts. Anglers call this "bass structure." The fish get comfortable with the **contour** of the lake bottom. At night, bass rest on the bottom of deeper waters, staying near logs or rocks.

Between meals, bass lounge near overhanging trees, piers, or brush. When they get hungry again, they start to prowl. The largemouth's schedule revolves around its next meal.

Diet

Largemouth bass stick to a daily routine. In early morning, they swim in deep waters of six to nine feet (1.8 to 2.7 meters). In the afternoon, they rest near their bass structure. At sundown, they start moving again, swimming in shallow water. When prey passes by, they strike.

Largemouth bass eat insects, frogs, crayfish, and worms. If they can get small mammals, birds, or snakes, down they go. There is one thing bass refuse to bite on and that is dead food.

Bass also swallow smaller fish, such as minnows, bluegill **fry**, and even their own young! A male largemouth will sometimes eat up to 90 percent of his offspring.

WILD FACTS!

Scientists learn about largemouth bass eating habits by studying the contents of their stomachs.

Largemouth bass in shallow water may become prey for large birds such as the heron.

In their own **habitats**, adult largemouth bass are top predators. They rarely become prey to other fish. At the top of the food chain, they have lots of choices. They eat almost anything!

Life Cycle

Largemouth bass **spawn** once a year. Spawning happens in March in southern waters and late May in the north. When the water warms to between 60 and 70 degrees Fahrenheit (15.6 and 21°C), it's time.

The male chooses a spot in 1 to 3 feet (0.3 to 1 m) of water about 10 feet (3 m) from the shore. On the sandy bottom, he anchors his nose and then swims in a circle. With his tail, he sweeps a clear, circular hollow. The nest has a **diameter** twice the length of his body.

When a female largemouth comes along, they swim together and he directs her to the nest. She releases eggs into the nest. Then, the male **fertilizes** them.

The female then swims away. The male stays and guards the eggs. He fans them, giving them oxygen and keeping **silt** off them. He will strike savagely at any fish that threaten the nest.

WILD FACTS!

If the water gets too cold, the male will leave the nest. The eggs never hatch. They become food for other fish.

If they are not taken by a predator, these largemouth fry will live about 13 years.

In seven to ten days, the eggs hatch. Warm water will cause the eggs to hatch more quickly. When they are about one inch (2.5 cm) long, the bass **fry** leave the nest.

Gone Fishing

Laws regulate the time of year largemouth bass may be caught. These restrictions protect the fish during their **spawning** season. This helps maintain a healthy bass population.

When it's time to go fishing, be sure to put safety first! Wear a hat, sunglasses, and even safety glasses when casting. In hot weather, apply sunscreen and insect spray. Keep a first-aid kit nearby. A flashlight, a knife, and a cell phone or radio are also handy.

Bass anglers can fish from boats and piers or by standing in shallow water. On or near water, always wear a life preserver. And to catch the smart largemouth, the right tackle is key.

A bass will burst out of the water to strike at a surface lure.

Bass can see colors as well as you can. Brightly colored plastic worms are good when fishing in murky water.

The correct combination of rod, reel, and bait can catch more fish. Basic rods are made of **graphite** and **fiberglass**. Important considerations when choosing a rod are sensitivity and weight. Baits that require continuous casting need a lighter-weight rod. Using a more sensitive rod lets the angler feel what is happening with the bait.

There are also different types of reels to choose from. Spincast reels work well with lightweight lures. They are easier to use in windy weather.

However, many professional bass anglers prefer baitcast reels. These reels give the angler better control of the lure. Baitcasters can get tangled, though, if the spools spin too fast. They are harder to handle in high winds or bad weather.

Now for the bait. Stick-baits and topwater lures disturb the surface of the water. Buzzbaits splash and gurgle. On spinnerbaits, a fringed "skirt" hides the hook. In the water, the spinning blade ripples and flashes,

WILD FACTS!

The world-record largemouth was caught in Georgia's Montgomery Lake in 1932. The 22-pound, 4-ounce (10-kg, 113-g) lunker measured 32.5 inches (82.5 cm) long and 28.5 inches (72.3 cm) around.

Americans spent $4 billion on freshwater fishing tackle in 2011.

attracting hungry bass. But sometimes, simple is best.
Many anglers claim plastic worms are the number one
bass lure.

Largemouth bass strike viciously at the right bait.
Anglers live for these moments. But remember, bass will
only eat living food. For a bass to bite, the lure needs to
look alive. So, bass bait should move!

Got One!

The fish is in the boat. Now what? If it is a possible record-breaker, keep it cool and wet. Do not clean or freeze the fish. Removing the hook quickly helps prevent tissue damage. Never set a fish on a hot, dry boat deck or pier.

Snap a picture! Weigh the fish as soon as possible. Find a certified scale in a bait shop, grocery store, or hardware store. Weight must be witnessed by an observer. Contact the nearest state wildlife office. They will positively identify the bass species.

Can you eat largemouth bass? Generally, bass are more a sport fish than a game fish. Younger ones, three pounds (1.4 kg) or smaller, are good grilled, fried, or

Anglers who practice catch and release still want to know the weight of their prize. So, they weigh the bass with a ruler! To estimate the weight of a fish, use this formula: (length x girth x girth) / 927 = bass weight

broiled. Older largemouths are less tasty.

So, many sport anglers practice catch and release. The sooner the fish is slipped back into the water, the better. Handle fish gently with wet hands, one on the lower jaw, and the other under the belly. Place the bass back into the water. Slowly move the fish back and forth to revive it. When the fish begins to move on its own, let go and watch it swim away.

Unlike some sports, with practice, fishing is a sport at which we all can excel.

Day's End

When the day is done, cleaning up keeps waters safe for everyone. Everything carried in must be carried out. Garbage can ruin a fishing spot. Fishing line in the trash or water can kill turtles and birds. Even gum wrappers can cause harm. Fish or birds may choke if they think the trash is food.

Never dump unused bait into the water. Many lakes have become infested with baitfish. They squeeze native fish out. Some **invasive** species are not visible to the naked eye. Deadly largemouth bass virus can easily spread from one body of water to another. So rinse gear, clothing, and boats before entering another body of water.

Sport fishing brings people together. Experienced anglers can teach beginners the ropes. Bass fishing tournaments are a popular way to sharpen skills. Being prepared and staying safe make fishing for largemouth bass fun!

The next record-breaking largemouth bass could be yours!

Glossary

bag limit - a usually daily limit on the number of fish an angler may keep.

calcified - hard or stiff as a result of calcium salts.

climate change - a long-term change in Earth's climate, or in that of a region of Earth. It includes changing temperatures, weather patterns, and more. It can result from natural processes or human activities.

contour - the general form or outline of something.

diameter - the distance across the middle of an object, such as a circle.

ecosystem - a community of organisms and their surroundings.

environment - all the surroundings that affect the growth and well-being of a living thing.

fertilize - to make fertile. Something that is fertile is capable of growing or developing.

fiberglass - glass in the form of fibers used for making various products.

fry - young fish that are not yet big enough to be fingerlings.

graphite - a soft, shiny, black form of carbon.

habitat - a place where a living thing is naturally found.

invasive - tending to spread.

lateral line - a sensory organ that runs along a fish's sides. It detects vibrations and changes in temperature and water pressure.

silt - fine sand or clay that is carried by water and deposited as sediment.

spawn - to produce or deposit eggs.

Web Sites

To learn more about largemouth bass, visit ABDO Publishing Company online. Web sites about largemouth bass are listed on our Book Links page. These links are routinely monitored and updated to provide the most current information available.
www.abdopublishing.com

Index